I0447603

I 'm Dead, Now What?

By

Wayne Hall

I'm Dead, Now What?

Copyright@2012 by Wayne Hall
For more information contact Wayne at:
www.waynelhall.com or
www.Iamdeadnowwhat.com

Praise for Wayne Hall's Work!

Reading this book is a transformation of good writing a must read! It claims our attention and emotional response because of the honesty and pain of life we endure. But I had to laugh, yeh mon! laugh"."Gimme back mi what's it not's it money" one can surely relate to author's experience having lost my mother and dear friend. And to see that one can share this information. A must read.

Lou Brown.
Founder of Island Blend Radio

This humorous take on death is unusual, but it captures how some people do feel about it. It's not always devastating.

Kinshasa Lindsay
Freshman at Georgia Gwinnett College

This book will not only help its readers to better handle the loss of a loved one to death; it will also show how wonderful it is when that loved one has left a legacy of love and preparedness. Wayne Hall in this book has definitely crafted a magnificent toolbox which includes items that build a smoother path as you make plans for the final arrangements. Read for information and fun. A great read.

Joan P. Lloyd-Granston M.Ed.
Doctoral Candidate, Walden University

A unique blend of storytelling and providing information. Grabs your attention and holds it all the way to the end. Very Intriguing. A must read.

Michelle Hanniford-Hall
Travel Agent/Payroll Specialist

Wayne captures the true essence of what it feels like to have a death in the family in Jamaica- although the examples highlighted in his book are of good use to everyone. Very humorous indeed, but it is goes beyond that-he makes you think and learn from his experience and knowledge.

A must read.

Sandy Daley, Author & Columnist.

Very typical of Wayne's ability to combine humor with the most serious of issues. Well documented, informative and entertaining. A must read.

Collin Henriques

Pastor (Church of God of Prophecy)

Dedication

To My wonderful family: Michelle, Waychelle and Chellayne, who in their own unique way influenced this work. To my mom Winnifred Hall who is undoubtedly the strongest black woman on the earth.

You have raised us to be proud and ambitious. You have withstood the ultimate pain of burying two kids and a husband, and have stood like a colossus through it all. To all my brothers and sisters with whom I have shared this journey of life. To friends, too numerous to mention, who have always been there, I thank you for all your love and support over the years.

To the memory of my father Donald Lloyd Hall, a man who epitomized the meaning of family. Lived it daily and who is the inspiration of this book in so many ways. In memory of my brothers, David Hall and Barrington Rowe, who both left too soon but lives on in my heart.

Foreword

"God pours life into death and death into life without a drop being spilled." Author Unknown

How appropriate the above words. Death as uncertain and sad as it is can if treated differently actually be a motivation to carry on for those left behind by a loved one. Who wants to think of death when the bright present we live in with all its hopes can only be spoiled by such a final and bone chilling thought. Facing our mortality is one of our toughest challenges as humans. It is such an irony that the most certain act of our existence is one that creates the most disturbing of emotions for us. It is an absolute art to be anywhere near being remotely calm when dealing with the death of a loved one. It cannot be taught or trained. In fact many have collapsed at the thought that their loved one has moved on.

Why then do we have to face such a horrible reality? Or should the question be, is death as horrible as we make it to be? Dealing with its challenges will either make or break you. On occasions that I have lost a loved one I cannot help but notice how the simplest of gestures by just about anyone helps to make it easier. Encouragement comes from all angles. Support in a country such as Jamaica can be in a card, some comforting words by mouth or an individual bringing you a bunch of green bananas. No act will bring back the deceased. However everything that occurs after their passing can make you want to just throw in the towel.

The individuals, groups and businesses that offer help during this time cannot be too sensitive to ones need at this moment of their life. A funeral home can be heaven sent, however if the service provider is not trained and on the spot with you it's like they are killing your loved one all over again.

Several events leading up to my dad's death helped to make it easier for me to take care of his funeral arrangements. Not many will have that luxury. A rainbow literally appeared out of nowhere on a dry sunny day the same day my dad passed. I took a photograph as I stood in our backyard looking at it. That picture also captured a banana tree. There is a reflection of strength in the banana tree and hope with the rainbow with what will hopefully be a pot of gold at the end. This oh so natural picture is in so many ways a reflection of the mixed up emotions one journeys through.

People die every day. It's the harsh reality we have to face. Funeral homes are very great for handling and helping you manage the loss of loved ones. Embrace the process and understand that it is as legal as it is emotional and is as character building as it is challenging. I hope that you will enjoy reading this literature.

"I 'm Dead Now What?' is simply my way of saying do not panic in the face of death. Let's step up and greet the challenges it brings with the knowledge that we are doing a loved one proud by performing his or her final rites thus giving them a sendoff they truly deserve. This book is dedicated to the memory of Donald Lloyd Hall. A man who as a father, was unrivalled in his dedication and commitment to his family. He took care of all the funerals easing every one of that burden. It is therefore not surprising that when he went it would stimulate the writing of this book. May his memories live forever. February eleven, nineteen thirty seven to January twenty seven, two thousand and twelve.

INTRODUCTION

"Dying is a part of living" Charles de Lint, The Little Country.

This book was inspired quite unexpectedly by the challenges of getting my dad's funeral arrangements handled in Jamaica.

It was a chilly morning as I departed Atlanta for Kingston Jamaica. As my friend drove me to the airport, we talked about the calming feeling it gives, to be aware of the spiritual aspect of life and death. I flew in from Atlanta and managed to see my dad before he passed. Getting to see him was my first reality check as far as navigating the different circumstances in Jamaica goes.

I was told at the hospital gate that I cannot see my ailing dad as I had just missed visiting hours. I tried to explain that I just spent an entire night awake trying to find a ticket so I could be there to see my dad alive. I had to go through three different individuals one of whom tried to articulate why it was more important for me to keep on rolling than it is for them to break the rules.

After much restraint and persuasion I was finally allowed to go inside. I had to ask the supervisor how would she feel to know I did all I could to see my dad alive and because of a lack of discretion on their part I failed to see him? Although, he was in a coma he saved the last response to anyone, for me. The second I began speaking and mentioned my name, his breathing quickened almost like that of an excited child. As I watched his chest rapidly expand and contract, he turned his head to me as if to say something but he was much too weak to articulate. At that moment I assured him that no matter what happened, just like Marley said "everything would be all right". I quietly went over all the concerns I knew we had discussed prior. In a strange way I felt his right hand which I held with my right hand convulse oh so gently. I now realize in a moment of revelation- as I write this that it was his final gesture, an actual hand shake. I returned to see him the next day and this time he had no response to my presence. Ten hours later I had the dreaded phone call. He had succumbed to his illness and bade goodbye.

It was a loud silence inside the nursing office of Ward five in the Spanish Town Hospital. With me was Doctor Powell the doctor who treated my dad last. He sighed heavily and was very compassionate and literally apologetic as he broke the sad news to my Stepbrother Collin and I. "We did all we could", he said chokingly. "I am sorry we could not have done more". We took it as strongly as we could. At the end of the briefing by Doctor Powell, I walked over to the side of his bed looked at his limp body and thought of how full of life he used to be. How in so many ways he was the reason so many lived. Yet, there he lay motionless, taking with him a life of thrills and spills, ups and downs and a mind as sharp as a razor.

As my brother and I drove home to break the news to Mom and my brothers and sisters we ventured on a journey of reflections. My dad and I often discussed death. We both had a liking for the saying "dying is a part of living". Oddly enough this phrase formed the basis on which I proceeded to coordinate my dad's funeral arrangements.

It was the process of handling his funeral that inspired this book. It would be churlish of me not to mention that other than the actual experience of coordinating the funeral, my wife is to be credited for this project. She stayed behind in Lawrenceville, GA (twenty two miles north of Atlanta) with our two daughters who were attending school while I was in Jamaica. After several calls to her outlining what the experience was like she told me I had to write this book. As a matter of fact she came up with the title also.

Coordinating a funeral in Jamaica can best be described as a journey. On some days it felt like a quantum leap and on others it at best could be described as retrogression. At times it felt like a pendulum swinging from the ridiculous to the sublime.

On my visit to the hospital for the medical certificate I was told I could not have it as my mother was listed as my dad's next of Kin. It was so ironic that my seventy five years old mother – not in the best of health herself would have to tackle these challenges. Fortunately after some quiet pleading and a call to my mom I was able to get it.

From there it was off to the department of birth and death in Spanish Town. Here is where it began to sink in how challenging the experience can be. The ladies recording my dad's death had a difficult time interpreting what the doctors wrote. I had to help her out much to her amazement. As if that was not enough, they brought me back the draft of the Death Certificate with my name as the deceased. We quickly overcame this hurdle then the next one sprung. I had to have exact change to pay for the certificate. The cashier could not find the change. I went to a restaurant on the facility, where they told me if I bought something they can assist me with the change. I ordered a lunch of rice and peas and fried chicken for my nephew who had accompanied me. As she was about to hand me the lunch I realized I was not being given the change for which I actually purchased the food. I politely asked her what had happened to the change she promised me? Then in a show of presumption bar none she cynically told me she would not have the change as she did not have exactly what I needed. Right there and then the journey swung from sublime to ridiculous. I quickly told her to hand me back my "what's it not's it money" and keep her food. I did not hesitate to offer her some cool advice on what she could do with the damn food.

Amazingly, I suddenly no longer seemed the fool she thought she had. As quickly as I increased my vocal decibel level was as quickly as she was handing me back my money. Next move was a trip outside the facility to the higglers on the side of the street. Believe it or not they were much more helpful than the restaurant on the facility itself. Happy to get change I went back in and had to join the line to the cashier again.

Right then I sensed what it was going to be like tackling these kinds of situations. It required much patience and calm. I soon received a burial order so I could now go and arrange a funeral. Wait a minute, my dad wanted to be cremated. On with the task, as I walked into the funeral home to give them the number on the burial order. With this number and the form to transfer my dad's body, they would now take his body from the home that removed it from the hospital where he died. I had to now swing by the first funeral home to identify my dad's body. This to make sure the funeral home of our choice received the correct body. The exchange cost ten thousand Jamaican dollars.

With his body now where we wanted it and burial order in hand it was time to start narrowing down the funeral arrangements. It was a blessing to work with the most helpful young lady at the funeral home. I met with her the Saturday after he passed and she outlined what needed to be done. She also gave me the relevant paperwork to be prepared so he could be cremated. With her guidance I was able to plan carefully and on time. In fact I was able to go back to the states for a week then return to wrap everything up for the Memorial Services and subsequent cremation.

As you read this book, I hope you will find this information extremely helpful. Death never occurs at the moment we would like. In fact it always seems to catch us totally off guard. This is intended to provide you with a framework within which to operate. Should you lose a loved one, please find a funeral home and discuss how they can assist you with the arrangement.

This book serves to compliment what you will find in a funeral home – not to replace what they can do for you. Having had four very close relatives pass on during a ten year period, under four totally different circumstances, I am strongly motivated to share these insights and hope that it helps to make the process less frustrating for you.

I 'M DEAD, NOW WHAT?

Managing The Funeral Arrangements of a loved one In Jamaica.

This is a look at the post death scenario in Jamaica. This book is intended to bring attention to the challenges of burying your loved one. The book is also intended to be a resource to those who will need to refer to it, but should also to be of intrigue to anyone who reads it.

As you read this please keep in mind it has been inspired by the writer's own experience as he coordinated his father's Funeral Service & Cremation. He has also lived through the passing of a forty five year old brother in a motor cycle accident, a thirty eight year old brother who collapsed and died and a grandma who died peacefully in her sleep at ninety one years old. It's amazing how all these deaths had their unique way of being handled due to the different set of circumstances involved. No two deaths are alike but by reading this literature hopefully one finds enough to serve as a useful guide through this necessary but far from pleasant role that life's journey takes us on.

HOW DID I DIE?

"To himself everyone is immortal; he may know that he is going to die, but he can never know that he is dead." Samuel Butler

The manner of death for any individual is as uncertain as death itself is certain. The only way to guarantee how you die is to plan and execute a successful suicide. This takes us to the first manner of death we will examine, that of suicide.

"They tell us that suicide is the greatest piece of cowardice…that suicide is wrong; when it is quite obvious that there is nothing in the world to which every man has a more unassailable title than to his own life and person". Arthur Schopenhauer

Suicide in itself is not final. It merely describes the fact that one has killed himself. He could kill himself by a gun shot, poisoning or hanging. However he chose to, you the relative will be left figuring out what to do to bury him. It must be reported to the police who will investigate. There will then be a post mortem to officially determine actual cause of death.

How else though could I have died? I could die from any other of the following:

-A prolonged illness such as cancer, lupus, hypertension, diabetes to name a few.

-        One can die suddenly from an accident, a heart attack; Gun shot wound or an aneurism. Death can occur very quickly; it can also be imminent but not occur for a period of time.

No matter what vehicle death arrives in, there is a follow up process that will be determined by a critical terminology. I'm referring to "Cause of Death". The cause of death can be the blue print for what takes place next as far as the process of taking care of the remains.

Of high importance also is the "Place of Death". Where one dies can have a huge impact on how their loved one will have to navigate the post death period. Places where one can die include but are not limited to dying as a tourist in a foreign country, dying at your local hospital. Death can occur on the way to a hospital, on a play ground, in a car or on the job. In many instances death occurs right at home.

WHEN DID I DIE?

"Watching a peaceful death of a human being reminds us of a falling star; one of a million lights in a vast sky that flares up for a brief moment only to disappear into the endless night forever". Elisabeth Kubler-Ross

Death can be an event in the womb, or even a few hours after being born, It can occur during infancy or as a toddler, teenager or during the adult years. According to psychological theories the different stages of life can be categorized as follows:

Early Childhood	0 – 8 years
Pre-Adolescent	9 – 13 years
Adolescent	13 – 19 years
Young Adult	20 – 40 years
Middle Adulthood	50- 60 years
Maturity	60 and older

Like everything else surrounding death the stage of life at which one dies can have a significant bearing on the steps that follows as far as the burial process is concerned.

Many questions often arise, such as was there a Will? Does the deceased own property? Who is next of kin; Are there any special post death requirements for instance, cremation?

Let me remind readers that the primary goal of this book is to provide insight into how loved ones can navigate the process of handling the death of a loved one in Jamaica. The ultimate goal is to save those grieving some time, money & to lessen the frustration commonly associated with the process.

All sorts of questions exist at this time. Is there a body? What do I do if there is not a body? If there is a body how can I get control of it? Upon receipt of the body how do I plan to take care of it? Will it be buried, Cremated or preserved? Can I legally cremate due to cause of death? Will there be an issue if I cremate vs bury? Each situation requires a different approach all with different circumstances. A simple act such as listing the wrong person as the next of kin can impact a tail spin on the post death process. Furthermore, providing inaccurate information can also be time consuming and lead to extreme levels of frustration.

Jamaica is indeed a very unique country for many reasons, including how different services and functions are executed and embraced. It is sometimes so laid back that the most basic protocol goes ignored, and only the very squeaky wheels get the grease. One can find that the simplest challenge is achieved by having to balance screaming, patience and persistent communication.

In fact there are many instances where frustration has lead to the prospect of bribery as a last resort. The question therefore is "Can one in a systematic way, efficiently handle the process of burying a loved one in Jamaica? The answer is "Yes", certainly!

By anticipating what the possibilities are and always thinking what's next, one can generate an order of events. By so doing, the encounter will be much easier. Once it is clear what needs to be done, the challenge now depends on who you're faced with for help and how the combination of their attitude and yours will break or make the experience.

The remainder of this book will outline different scenarios and seek to shed light on how best to proceed in each.

DYING AT A HOSPITAL

"Time rushes towards us with its hospital tray of infinitely varied narcotics, even while it is preparing us for its inevitably fatal operation".
Tennessee Williams, "The Rose Tattoo"

If your loved one dies at a hospital after being hospitalized for a while you will have a simpler than usual process. Following their passing here are the steps to take:

1. Ascertain who was listed as next of kin. It is important that the next of kin listed, be able-bodied, mobile and very physically and emotionally capable of managing the immediate requirements. The next of kin must then visit the Birth and Death department at the hospital to receive a medical Certificate of Death filled out by the attending physician. Should the listed next of kin be incapable he/she must write a note to the person substituting on their behalf at the hospital.

2. Upon receipt of the medical Certification of Death, find a copy center usually at a book store or internet Café and make at least three copies.

3. The next stop should be to the Registrar General's office for Birth and Death and Marriages at Twickenham Park in Spanish Town. Twickenham Park, St. Catherine is the main operation and its eight branch offices are in the parishes of Kingston and St. Andrew, Manchester, St. Elizabeth, Westmoreland, St. James, St. Ann, Portland and Clarendon. They can be contacted via email at

information@**rgd.gov**.jm. They can be
contacted via telephone from eight thirty AM
to five PM during the day Mondays-Fridays.
They can also be reached at night by
telephone between nine PM and five AM. The
numbers to call are 876-749-0550 or 876-619-
1260. Here you're able to register the death
officially and receive a burial order. In
exchange of the Medical Certificate you will
receive a pink form known as the burial order.
It is a very important document. Make three
copies of it also.

4. Pay close attention to the paperwork before
   signing off on it while at the registry. Several
   mistakes have occurred there and require a
   tedious process known as "**Correction of
   Error**" to fix it. As I previously mentioned I was
   named on the certificate as the deceased.
   Luckily I caught it.

5. Think of which Funeral Home you want to
   work with. Shop around for the one with the
   package that best suits your needs. Take the
   burial order to them and have an official
   meeting to start the process of burial. In many
   cases the government has contracts for a
   specific funeral home to receive the dead from
   their hospitals. If you decide to use a Funeral
   Home other than the one that retained the
   body from the hospital, they will need you to
   approve a transfer of the body. Upon
   receiving the Medical Certificate for cause of
   death, you will also receive a document that
   allows you to legally have the body transferred
   to you or the Funeral home you wish to use.
   Be sure to ask for this piece of document.

6. Be prepared to identify the body to ensure the body of your loved one is indeed the body you receive.

7. Once you are in possession of the body, you can begin to make funeral arrangements with relatives, friends and the Funeral home.

WHAT TO DO IF THE LOVED ONE REQUESTED, OR YOU DECIDE TO CREMATE

"The death of someone we know always reminds us that we are still alive – perhaps for some purpose which we ought to re-examine". Mignon Mclaughlin, The Neurotic's Notebook, 1960

If you plan to cremate here is a suggested guideline to follow:

1.   As soon as the loved one passes consult with the funeral home you plan to use and ask for guideline with the process. They will give you a set of paperwork that must be filled out and returned before the cremation can take place.

The paper work is as follows:

a. One form for the next of kin and JP to complete

b. A form that must be completed by the last doctor that treated the deceased. It consists of two pages.

c. The ministry of health in the area where he died must fill out a form also. Here you will be asked to pay a fee. In February two thousand and twelve this fee was two thousand Jamaican dollars.

d. The final set of paper must be completed by the Superintendent of Police in the area where he passed. Be advised that the Superintendent is the last stop in the process. Make sure when you get to the Superintendent office you have two copies of all the completed paperwork, including the receipt for payment at the MOH. They will need a copy also of the medical certificate of death and the original burial order (pink slip). If by this time you have received a true Certificate of death you can use this instead of the copy of the medical certificate of death.

Once the superintendent checks and signs off on the paperwork you will get it back with the document to take to the funeral home. The funeral home will make copies of the originals and give them back to you. They will however hold onto the burial order until after the cremation. Upon completion of the cremation you will get back the stamped burial order along with a certificate of cremation. These usually accompany the urn containing the remains of the deceased.

After a burial the burial order must be signed by the officiating minister at the funeral service and returned ASAP to the Registrar General.

WHAT IF THE PERSON DIES AT HOME?

"As a well – spent day brings happy sleep, so a life well used brings happy death". Leonardo da Vinci

Should someone pass at home the police must be summoned. Upon arrival the police will carry out an investigation to ensure no foul play is suspected. Should foul play be suspected they will collect all relevant evidence from the scene and a post mortem is required. Upon completion of this initial investigation the body is then brought to a nearest hospital or medical facility where it is officially pronounced dead. If a post mortem is required to determine cause of death the loved ones must wait before proceeding with burial or cremation arrangements.

 If a post mortem has to be performed here is an overview of the process.

The police that removed the body will complete a form requesting the post mortem to be done. He will then receive a confirmation from the pathology unit that will do the post mortem. There will be notice given by the unit as to the date and time the post mortem is scheduled for. A family member or next of kin of the deceased will need to confirm the identification of the deceased prior to the post mortem. Upon completion of the post mortem a burial order is issued to the relative or next of kin. This will allow the family to plan the funeral. After the funeral the officiating pastor must fill out the burial order which can then be used to officially register the death within a two to three month window.

Accidental Death

"Death is beautiful when seen to be law and not an accident - It is as common as life". Henry David Thoreau, 11 March 1842, letter to Ralph Waldo Emerson

In case of sudden death and Accidental death the process starts with an investigation. Once this is complete there will be a decision whether to do a post mortem or not. If a post mortem be deemed necessary. Follow post mortem procedure in previous chapter.

Burial Preparations

"Someday I'll be a weather-beaten skull resting on a grass pillow, serenaded by a stray bird or two. Kings and commoners end up the same, no more enduring than last night's dream".
Ryokan

First and foremost is **WHERE** will the burial take place? This will have to be answered swiftly. Once the designated area has been identified the arrangements for digging of the grave comes next. Many are sub-contracting this out these days to lessen the hassle that comes with it. Jamaican tradition dictates that those participating in the digging must be fed and served alcohol throughout the time it takes to do so. These days many funeral homes are including this aspect as part of their packages.

Money Worries

"Death is the surest calculation that can be made". Ludwig Buchner, Force and Matter

At the center of everything is the need for the almighty dollar/s. A funeral undertaking can be quite expensive. Often the first words out of one's mouth is "lawd wheh mi gwine find money fi bury mi dead?" Where will the money come from? Depending on your loved ones status at the time of death you may have some options for money. Key questions are does the deceased have life insurance. Has the deceased left enough to afford a burial or cremation? Can the dead be buried and the relatives afford to live on what remains after the funeral has been paid for? Did the deceased have a bank account and are the funds accessible.

Options include the following. Check with The NIS office in your region to see if you can receive a funeral grant. Typically one will receive a grant of seventy thousand Jamaican dollars to assist with the expenses. Unfortunately you must bury the deceased first then present the NIS office with a copy of the receipt from the funeral home in order to receive this grant.

Check with the last place of employment to see if there was a funeral plan for the deceased. Many companies actually have accounts that employees can participate in. These accounts guarantee them a certain amount towards a funeral at the time of their passing. Some credit unions and investment companies offer a funeral loan against the amount they have saved or investing in their company.

If the deceased leaves behind a bank account that was a joint account, the relative or individual listed on the account will be required to present a death certificate in order to close out the account. Of course that person can withdraw all the money needed. One option to keep in mind where the bank is concerned is that you can request a check made out to the funeral home directly from the bank. They will pay this out against the remaining balance in the account. If you want to add another person to an account from which someone deceased, remember to take the death certificate to prove that the previous joint holder is dead and you need to close that account and open a new one with the other person you now wish to add as a joint holder.

When one is depending on a life insurance payout to cover the death expenses, there are some steps to keep in mind. Be sure to contact the insurance company on how to proceed with the death claim. They will let you know what paperwork is needed and what your options are. In a case where there is a post mortem some insurance companies will actually have you take their version of the death certificate to the doctor who performs the autopsy to fill it out. This will suffice in lieu of the actual death certificate which will be received when the death is officially registered at an office of the registrar's office of birth death and marriage. In general the forms required by the Insurance company are:

- Policy Contract
- Death Certificate showing the cause of death
- Claimants Statement also known as the death claim
- Claim Discharge form
- Identification

Please note that if you reside abroad you can have these forms sent to you so you can fill them out and have them notarized. Please also have your passport or ID picture notarized and you can then send these off to get the process started. The key is to contact the insurance company and follow their guide.

Finally we can always depend on the contributions of friends and relatives. Although it may not be enough to cover all the costs involved, family and friend donations go a long way in easing some of the financial burdens involved with the cost of dying.

When all is said and done though discuss your financial situation with the funeral home. Many funeral homes will bury the deceased and await the payout from a life insurance policy and/or the NIS office.

Conclusion

By now you must be saying wow I did not know it could get so difficult when one dies. Yes there is a true cost of dying and those left to deal with it can be financially, emotionally and physically worn out by the time it's over. Remaining calm is the number one step in navigating the process. You want your loved one to have the best sendoff ever while not breaking the bank in the process. There are several routes one can take. One must however not be afraid to ask questions and ask for others to help in every way possible. There is no clear cut prescribed way to handle a funeral process. So many variables make every situation different. I would like to leave you the reader with some reminders of key items in the process.

1. Find a funeral Home and ask all possible questions. Then trust and pray that God will guide you through it all.

2. Check on financial position of the deceased. Is the dead entitled to grants from the government or employers especially if he or she dies while working? Many companies pay a life insurance on employees.

3. Be sure to find out if the deceased had any special requests about how they want to be buried or cremated etc.

4. Try to be calm and patient especially when dealing with the different Government regulated steps involved.

5. Immediately make at least two copies of all death related documents.

6. Pay close attention to the details on the death certificate and all other documents for that matter. You do not want to overlook an error and it bites you in the butt later.

7. Always try to stay one step ahead of the process.

8. No question is too dumb and help cannot be too much. Ask questions and ask for help. For example based on cause of death you may be held up due to a post mortem. Find out if there will be one and when so you can plan accordingly especially if you are going to be traveling from abroad.

9. Do not overdo the process just to try and please friends and some family members. For example feeling pressured to pay a band and/or to kill a cow.

Finally treat the process as one of honor on behalf of the deceased. It's the last opportunity to do the dead a favor. Send them off in style.

"I'm Dead Now What?" has hopefully provided some guidance to the process of handling a loved one's funeral. It may not have hit every nail on the head. What I hope it has done is provided a framework. A framework that has left you feeling much calmer and at ease knowing that it's a process and that with calm, patience and carefully anticipating every step the deceased will have a marvelous sendoff.

"If the people we love are stolen from us, the way to have them live on is to never stop loving them. Buildings burn, people die, but real love is forever".
The Crow, written by James O'Barr, David J. Schow, and John Shirley, 1994.

I'm Dead, Now What?